Using Flannelboards to Teach
Readiness Skills

written by Marsha Elyn Wright

illustrated by Patty McCloskey

Grade Pre-K – First Grade

Editors: Stephanie Oberc-Garcia
Robert Newman
Art Director: Rita Hudson
Cover Design: Joanne Caroselli
Book Design: Shelly Brown
Graphic Artist: Carol Arriola

Cover Photography by Color Inc.

J330001 Using Flannelboards to Teach Readiness Skills
All rights reserved—Printed in the U.S.A.
Copyright © 2000 Judy/Instructo
A Division of Frank Schaffer Publications, Inc.
23740 Hawthorne Blvd., Torrance, CA 90505

Table of Contents

Tips for Cutouts and Flannelboards

Use flannelboards to help children develop reading readiness skills such as matching, left-to-right progression, visual discrimination, sight-word recognition, and letter-sound recognition. When young children interact with a flannelboard, their learning comes alive! These simple ideas will help you create cutouts and flannelboards for the many activities in this book.

Fabric Cutouts

Make cutouts from felt, flannel, or other fabric using your own shapes or using the easy-to-trace patterns in the back of this book. Photocopy the pattern pages you want to use, and then cut apart the patterns. Choose the color of fabric for each pattern. Secure the pattern on top of the fabric piece by pinning or taping the pattern to the fabric. Cut around the outer edge of the solid outline to create the shape. Or trace around the pattern using a black felt-tip marker to create a bold outline, and then cut out the shape. There are also manufactured felt cutouts of letters, numbers, basic geometric shapes, and other shapes available at teacher supply stores and craft stores. You can buy fabric that has a holiday- or theme-oriented pattern and make cutouts out of the fabric pictures.

Paper Cutouts

Trace stencils to make cutouts of letters, numbers, and shapes to use with a flannelboard. Use colorful calendar cutouts or cut out illustrations from coloring books and old workbooks! Just glue a piece of felt, sandpaper, or the "hooks" portion of self-sticking Velcro to the back of each cutout. The patterns in the back of this book also create sturdy paper cutouts. Before cutting the patterns apart, laminate the pages, cover them in clear self-stick paper, or photocopy them on different colors of tagboard or thick construction paper.

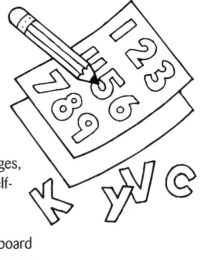

Storing Cutouts

Store your cutouts inside a resealable plastic bag. Label the bag with the name of the activity and, if appropriate, the page number where it can be found in this book. Place your storage bags in an expandable folder or box. You can also store your cutouts inside a manila folder by stapling both sides of the folder to form a large pocket. Label these folders and file them alphabetically by the title of the activity for a handy reference. You may want to use large envelopes to store your cutouts. This type of storage fits easily in filing cabinets and on shelves.

Making Flannelboards

You can purchase a manufactured flannelboard or try one of these ideas to create your own!

- **_Flat Carpet Flannelboard_**—Cut out a large rectangle or circle of felt or flannel. When you're doing a flannelboard activity, lay the fabric on your classroom carpet and have the children sit around it.

- **_Flat Box Flannelboard_**—Open and lay out flat a large cardboard box. Spray adhesive on the front. Place a large piece of felt or flannel on the front and smooth out the fabric from the center to the edges. (Attaching a thin layer of foam under the flannel works even better!) Good boxes to use include large pizza boxes, shipping boxes for large pictures, and packing boxes for posters.

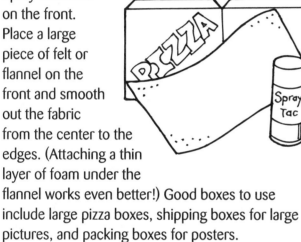

- **_Big Box Flannelboard_**—Spray adhesive on each side of a large box. Cut out felt or flannel pieces to match the dimensions of the sides of the box. Lay each piece on one side of the box and smooth out the fabric from the center to the edges. As you do an activity, use each side of your flannelboard box to display felt shapes.

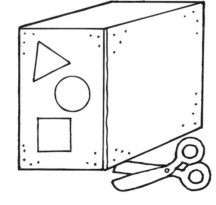

- **_Small Flannelboard_**—Glue a piece of felt or flannel around a small, lap-sized piece of laminate or sturdy cardboard; cover both sides. These small flannelboards make perfect lap-sized flannelboards for young children.

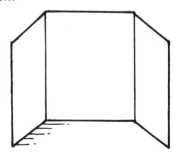

- **_Pressboard or Foamcore Flannelboard_**—Buy a large piece (at least 24" x 36") of pressboard or lightweight foamcore, either of which is available at art supply stores. Cut a length of felt or flannel that is about two inches larger on all sides than the board. Spray the front of the board with a spray adhesive. Lay the fabric on the board, leaving a two-inch overlap on all sides. Smooth out the fabric from the center to the edges. Then fold the edges back so that each corner forms a point on the back of the board. Cut off any excess fabric to leave neat corners; then use masking tape or glue to adhere the fabric to the back of the board.

- **_Folding Flannelboard_**—Collect two large pieces of sturdy cardboard. Cut one piece in half. Use masking tape to attach the smaller pieces to the left and right sides of the larger piece of cardboard to form two flaps. Spray adhesive on the front of the board. Lay a large piece of felt or flannel over the adhesive and smooth out the fabric from the center to the edges. Use the eraser end of a pencil to press and crease each fold so the flaps still bend. This flannelboard is perfect for displaying on a table when in use and folds up easily for quick storage.

Matching

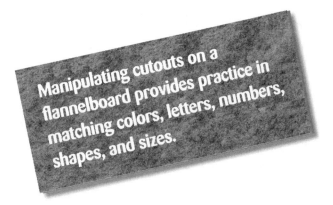

Manipulating cutouts on a flannelboard provides practice in matching colors, letters, numbers, shapes, and sizes.

Me and My Shadow

Visual discrimination, matching shapes

Materials: flannelboard, white piece of fabric about same size as flannelboard, variety of cutouts (pattern pages 52–64)

Prepare for this activity by laying the cutouts on the white fabric and using a black marker to trace each shape on the fabric. Add wiggly eyes to the animal cutouts. Use fabric paint to make details on the cutouts.

Place the white fabric on the flannelboard. Spread out the cutouts on the floor. Let the children take turns matching a cutout with its "shadow" by placing the corresponding cutout on top of the outline. As a follow-up activity, take the children outside to create shapes and shadows in the sunshine!

Silly Socks

Visual discrimination, matching designs

Materials: flannelboard, pairs of sock shapes cut from a variety of fabrics with theme-oriented patterns (one pair for each child)

Give each child one sock shape from a pair of socks. Place the remaining socks on the flannelboard. Point to one of the socks. Ask the children this question: *Who has the matching sock?* Let that child place his or her sock beside its match. Repeat this activity. This time, without pointing to a sock, let the children take turns finding their matching socks!

Alphabet Soup

Letter recognition, visual discrimination, matching uppercase letters

Materials: flannelboard, two sets of uppercase letter cutouts, large fabric "soup pot" shape

Spread out one set of letters on the floor. Place the "soup pot" on the flannelboard. Tell the children you will need their help in making alphabet soup. Explain that you are going to place the ingredients for the soup on the flannelboard. List the ingredients by placing about 10 alphabet letters in a column on the flannelboard. When you're finished, let the children take turns "reading" the ingredients and finding the matching letters from the floor. As each matching letter is found, it is placed "in" the pot on the flannelboard. As a follow-up, serve alphabet soup for a yummy treat. You'll be delighted with how many children try to identify the letters in their own soup!

Shape Robots

Visual discrimination, shape recognition, matching shapes and sizes

Materials: flannelboard; two sets of fabric squares, triangles, rectangles, and circles in varying sizes

Make a robot on the flannelboard using one set of fabric shapes. Spread out the other set of shapes on the floor. Let the children take turns matching each shape from the floor with a shape in the robot. Have each child place a shape on top of its match. Try this activity again. This time let the children take turns building the robot with one set of shapes!

Pairs of Squares

Visual discrimination, matching sizes

Materials: flannelboard, pairs of fabric squares cut in varying sizes

Randomly place one square from each pair on the flannelboard. Spread out the rest of the squares on the floor. Let the children take turns matching the pairs of squares. When a child sees a match, he or she places the square from the floor on top of its match on the flannelboard.

Jelly Beans

Matching colors

Materials: flannelboard, piece of fabric cut in the shape of a large jar, two sets of fabric jelly bean shapes in a variety of colors

Place the jar on the flannelboard. Randomly place some jelly beans from one set on the jar. Spread out the other set of jelly beans on the floor. Let the children take turns placing a jelly bean from the floor on top of its match in the jar. Repeat this activity by letting the children take turns "filling" the jar with jelly beans!

Creeping Caterpillar

Matching patterns

Materials: flannelboard, two sets of fabric circles in a variety of solid colors, one larger fabric circle, pipe cleaners, wiggly eyes, fabric paint

Use the larger circle for the caterpillar's head. Attach wiggly eyes and use fabric paint to make other facial details. Attach pipe cleaner antennae. Place the head on the flannelboard. Using one set of circles, make the caterpillar's body. Spread out the other set of circles on the floor. Let the children take turns placing a circle from the floor on top of its match on the caterpillar's body. Repeat this activity. This time let the children take turns creating a creeping caterpillar.

Letter Puzzles

Matching uppercase and lowercase letters

Materials: flannelboard, mini-sentence strips, self-sticking Velcro

For each letter of the alphabet, print an uppercase letter and its matching lowercase letter on a mini-sentence strip. Cut each strip in half using a simple curved, wavy, or zigzag line. Attach a "hooks" piece of Velcro to the back of each half. Randomly put some of the uppercase letter strips on the flannelboard. Spread out the lowercase letter strips on the floor. Let the children take turns finding a matching lowercase letter and putting it together with its uppercase match! Repeat this activity several times. Choose different children to place one half of a letter puzzle on the flannelboard and let him or her pick someone to find its match!

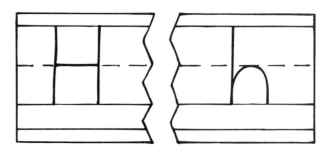

Color Worms

Matching patterns, color recognition

Materials: flannelboard, narrow strips of fabric, two sets of tiny fabric squares in a variety of solid colors

Arrange a pattern of squares and glue them on a strip of fabric to create a color worm. Make several more worms in different patterns. Then make another set of color worms that corresponds to the first set. Place one set of color worms on the flannelboard. Spread out the other set on the floor. Let the children take turns choosing a color worm on the floor and placing it on top of its match on the flannelboard. Repeat this activity again and again. Encourage the children to name the colors in each worm!

The Cookie Jar

Matching shapes and designs

Materials: flannelboard; piece of fabric cut in the shape of a large jar; two sets of fabric cookie shapes—stars, ovals, squares, diamonds, animals; long rectangles in a variety of fabrics

Place the jar on the flannelboard. Randomly place some cookies from one set "in" the jar. Spread out the other set of cookies on the floor. Let the children take turns placing a cookie from the floor on top of its match in the jar. Repeat this activity by letting the children take turns "filling" the cookie jar! As an extension activity, let the children count together the number of cookies in the jar before finding all the matches.

Whole/Part Relationships

Help young children develop their visual discrimination and thinking skills as they arrange parts to create a whole.

Funny Photos

Whole/part relationships, oral language

Materials: flannelboard, self-sticking Velcro, colorful photographs from old calendars and magazines, tagboard

Glue each photograph to a piece of tagboard to make a sturdy picture. Cut each picture into at least four vertical strips. Attach a "hooks" piece of Velcro to the back of each strip. Place one set of strips on the flannelboard so that the picture is scrambled. Let the children help you  rearrange the strips to form the correct picture. After the picture is assembled, ask the children questions about the picture such as the following: *What do you see happening in this picture? What do you think this person/animal is doing? Do you think this person/animal is happy or sad? What do you think will happen next?*

Broken Hearts

Whole/part relationships

Materials: flannelboard, several heart cutouts in varying sizes and colors (pattern page 52)

Cut each heart in half using a simple curved, wavy, or zigzag line. Place one half of each heart on the flannelboard. Spread out the remaining halves on the floor. Have the children take turns "mending the broken hearts." Let the children put together the matching hearts. This activity will be a popular one, especially near Valentine's Day!

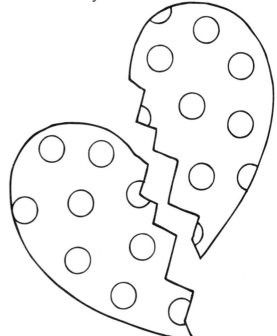

Going on an Egg Hunt

Whole/part relationships

> **Materials:** flannelboard, large fabric egg shapes in a variety of fabrics, several strips of green fabric

Cut each egg in half using a simple curved, wavy, or zigzag line. Place the green strips of fabric randomly in clusters on the flannelboard to represent tufts of grass. Then hide one half of each egg in a tuft of grass. Make part of the egg sticking out of the grass so that it's easily seen. Spread out the remaining halves on the floor. Have the children take turns hunting for the hidden egg halves. Let the children put together the matching eggs. What a fun activity for springtime!

Crayon Colors

Whole/part relationships, color recognition

> **Materials:** flannelboard, several crayon cutouts in different colors (pattern page 52)

Cut each crayon cutout in half using a simple curved, wavy, or zigzag line. Place one half of each crayon on the flannelboard. Spread out the remaining halves on the floor. Let the children take turns putting the matching halves together. Repeat this activity, encouraging the children to name the colors of the crayons.

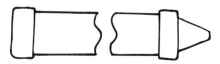

The Mouse's Moral

Whole/part relationships

> **Materials:** flannelboard; enlarge the elephant cutout (pattern page 52); *Seven Blind Mice* by Ed Young (Scholastic, 1992)

Use fabric paint, a wiggly eye, and yarn to add details to the elephant. Then cut the elephant into a few pieces. Randomly place the pieces on the flannelboard. Challenge the children to help you arrange the pieces into a definite shape, object, or animal. (Try to get the children to "see" the elephant.) Once the children have accomplished putting together the whole elephant, read aloud the delightful tale *Seven Blind Mice*. The end of the story is especially appropriate for this whole/part relationship activity. You and the children will delight in reading the mouse's moral!

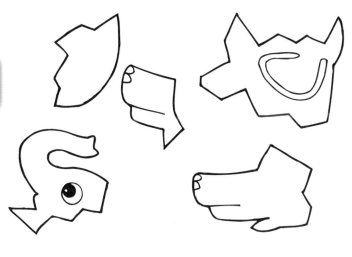

Left-to-Right Progression

Manipulating cutouts on the flannelboard helps children internalize left-to-right progression —a concept young children need as they get ready to read.

Sunday Comics

Left-to-right progression

Materials: flannelboard; simple, child-oriented Sunday comic strips; tagboard; self-sticking Velcro

Glue each comic strip to a length of tagboard to make a sturdy story. Attach a "hooks" piece of Velcro to the back of each strip. Place a comic strip on the flannelboard. As you read the captions, point to each illustration, reinforcing left-to-right order.

Funny Little Elephant

Left-to-right progression, oral language

Materials: flannelboard, three elephant cutouts (pattern page 52), four fabric trees, one small fabric circle, one small fabric diamond shape

Attach a wiggly eye to each elephant and add other details with fabric paint. Attach a yarn tail. Set up a scene on the flannelboard in left-to-right progression for each line of the following rhyme. For the first line, place one of the elephants on a tree. For the second line, place one elephant with the circle "ball" on a tree. For the third line, place one elephant with the diamond "kite" on a tree. For the last line, just have a fabric tree. Recite the rhyme and point to each illustration from left to right. Repeat this activity and let some children take turns pointing to the illustrations while the rest of the children recite the rhyme!

Funny little elephant sat upon a tree,
Funny little elephant tossed a ball with glee.
Funny little elephant sailed a purple kite,
Funny little elephant disappeared from sight!

Jack, Jump Over

Left-to-right progression

Materials: flannelboard; boy cutout (pattern page 58); candlestick, chick, and dog cutouts (pattern page 53); red fabric rectangle

Use wiggly eyes and fabric paint to add details to the cutouts. Place the cutouts in left-to-right order on the flannelboard. Teach the children the following rhyme. Let the children take turns making Jack jump over the items mentioned in the verses.

Jack, be nimble,
Jack, be quick,
Jack, jump over,
The candlestick!

Jack, be nimble,
Jack, be quick,
Jack, jump over,
The bright red brick!

Jack, be nimble,
Jack, be quick,
Jack, jump over,
The baby chick!

Jack, be nimble,
Jack, be quick
Jack, jump over,
The dog named Nick!

Mom and Dad Went Shopping

Color and shape recognition, visual discrimination

Materials: flannelboard, five mini-sentence strips, self-sticking Velcro, five different cutouts that could be birthday presents for a child (pattern pages 52–64), adult male and female cutouts (pattern page 58)

Use wiggly eyes, yarn, and fabric paint to add details to each cutout. Print *Monday, Tuesday, Wednesday, Thursday,* and *Friday* on separate mini-sentence strips. Attach a "hooks" piece of Velcro to the back of each strip. Place the strips in left-to-right order on the flannelboard. Have the children say the name of each  day as you point to it. Randomly place the cutouts on the flannelboard. Recite the rhyme. Let the children help choose each item bought. Have them take turns placing the appropriate item under the corresponding shopping day. Once the children learn this rhyme, have them recite it while other children pretend to be Mom and Dad shopping. Let "Mom and Dad" choose which items to purchase and place them under the appropriate days.

Mom and Dad went shopping,
For my birthday this week.
*On **Monday** they bought a(n)_____,*
I want to take a peek!

Mom and Dad went shopping,
For my birthday this week.
*On **Tuesday** they bought a(n)_____,*
I want to take a peek! (and so on)

Visual Discrimination

Flannelboard activities are perfect ways to help children develop the ability to see likenesses and differences.

Colors and Shapes

Color and shape recognition, visual discrimination

Materials: flannelboard; pairs of fabric circles, squares, triangles, ovals, and rectangles in a variety of colors

Use fabric paint to add simple designs on pairs of shapes. Remember to make the same design on both shapes so the pairs match. Randomly place one set of fabric shapes on the flannelboard. Spread out the other set of fabric shapes on the floor. Let the children take turns finding shapes and designs that pair up with those on the flannelboard. When a pair is found, place the shapes side by side.

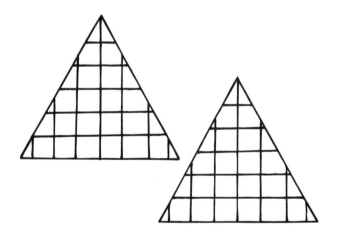

Funny Faces

Visual discrimination

Materials: flannelboard, 12 pairs of solid-color fabric circles

Use wiggly eyes, yarn, and fabric paint to make two each of six different funny faces on the circles. Place six different faces on the flannelboard. Place the other set of six faces on the floor. Let the children take turns matching up the pairs of faces. As an extension activity, encourage the children to talk about the faces. Ask the children questions such as the following: *Do you think this is a happy face or a sad face? If this was your face, what might you be feeling or thinking?*

Flannelboard BINGO

Visual discrimination, uppercase letter recognition

Materials: flannelboard, two sets of uppercase letter cutouts, large fabric squares (one for each child)

Choose 16 letters from one set of cutouts. Place the letters in a grid (four letters across and four letters down) on the flannelboard. Put the matching 16 letters from the second set of cutouts inside a box or bowl. Give each child a fabric square. Randomly pick a letter from the second set of cutouts and hold it up for the children to see. Ask the children: *What letter is this?* Choose a child to place his or her square over the corresponding letter on the flannelboard. When the last letter is covered, everyone shouts "BINGO!"

Something's Fishy

Visual discrimination

Materials: flannelboard, several pairs of fish cutouts (pattern page 54), large sheet of light blue felt

Decorate each pair of fish identically using wiggly eyes and fabric paint. Lay the blue felt on the bottom half of the flannelboard to represent water. Randomly place one fish from each pair "in the water." Spread out the remaining fish on the floor. Let the children "go fishing." Have them take turns placing the pairs together!

While a child goes "fishing," have the rest of the children chant this fun rhyme together:

Fishy, fishy, in the lake,
What a splash you can make!
Fishy, fishy, do not hide,
Jump into my arms so wide!

Building Houses

Visual discrimination

Materials: flannelboard; two sets of large fabric triangles, squares, and rectangles in a variety of colors

Tell the children you need their help to build houses. First, "build" a row of houses using one set of shapes. For each house, place a triangle roof over a rectangle or a square. (For example, a red roof triangle over a blue square or a green roof triangle over a brown rectangle.) Then challenge the children to "build" an identical row of houses.

Fancy Hearts

Visual discrimination, counting

Materials: flannelboard, 12 heart cutouts (pattern page 52)

Make pairs of fancy hearts. Use lace, ribbon, and fabric paint to decorate pairs of hearts identically. Place one of each pair of hearts on the flannelboard. Have the children look at the hearts and answer questions such as the following: *How is this heart different from that heart? How are these two hearts alike?* After the children begin to understand similarities and differences, spread out the remaining hearts on the floor. Let the children take turns placing the pairs together.

Number Jumble

Number recognition, visual discrimination

Materials: flannelboard, two sets of number cutouts (1–10)

Randomly place both sets of numbers on the flannelboard. Tell the children that the numbers are all jumbled up! Challenge them to find pairs of numbers. Let the children take turns placing the pairs together.

Take a Bow!

Visual discrimination, letter and name recognition

Materials: flannelboard, uppercase and lowercase letter cutouts

Using the letter cutouts, spell one of the children's names on the flannelboard. See if the children can recognize each letter and whose name the letters spell. Then teach the children the rhyme below. Fill in the blanks with the name of the child you spelled on the flannelboard. Have that child act out the words while the rest of the children chant the rhyme. Repeat the activity so that each child has a chance to perform!

_____, _____ walk around,
_____, _____ touch the ground.
_____, _____ show us how,
To stand up tall and take a bow!

You're in the Doghouse

Visual discrimination, color recognition

Materials: flannelboard, dog and doghouse cutouts in various solid colors (a solid color dog should match each solid color doghouse; pattern page 53)

Place the doghouses on the flannelboard. Spread out the dogs on the floor. Let the children take turns placing a dog by the doghouse of the same color. Try the activity again, but this time let the children take turns pairing up dogs and doghouses using different colors. Say to the children: *Place the red dog with the blue doghouse.*

Visual Memory

These flannelboard activities will help young children develop the ability to remember what they see and to identify what is missing from what was seen.

No Peeking!

Visual memory

Materials: flannelboard; heart, crayon, and elephant cutouts (pattern page 52); dog and chick cutouts (pattern page 53); fish cutout (pattern page 54); large fabric rectangle

Place three cutouts on the flannelboard and cover them with the rectangle. Tell the children that you are going to let them peek under the "box" to see what's inside of it. Lift up the rectangle for a minute. After replacing the rectangle, ask the children to name the items inside the box. Choose a child to peek inside again and check to see if the items named are the items in the box. Repeat this activity several times using different cutouts. Challenge the children by placing more than three cutouts under the rectangle.

The Animal Tree

Visual memory

Materials: flannelboard, fabric tree, various animal cutouts (pattern pages 52–61), large sheet of fabric that can cover the tree

Arrange the tree in the middle of the flannelboard. Place some animals in the tree and some under the tree. Ask the children these kinds of questions: *Which animals are in the tree? How many animals are under the tree? What are their names?* Then cover the tree with the sheet of fabric. Ask the children to tell you which animals are hidden. Challenge the children to name only the animals in the tree or only the animals under the tree!

Baby Teeth

Counting, visual memory

Materials: flannelboard; several tooth cutouts (pattern page 54); red fabric cut into the shape of a wide, smiling mouth

Place some teeth on the flannelboard. Cover them with the "smile." Lift up the mouth and have the children count together how many teeth are shown. Tell the children that some of the baby teeth are loose. Remove one or more teeth. Cover the teeth again. Challenge the children to remember how many teeth remain under the smile! This activity is so much fun that the children will want to do it again and again.

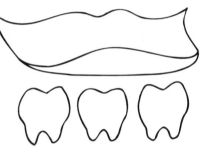

Flying in the Clouds

Visual memory, color recognition

Materials: flannelboard, airplane cutouts in solid colors (pattern page 54), large white fabric cloud shape

Place a few airplanes on the flannelboard. Let the children name the colors together. Then cover the airplanes with the cloud. See how many children can name the hidden colors.

Hatching Lizards

Visual memory, color recognition

Materials: flannelboard, lizard cutouts in solid colors (pattern page 54), large white fabric egg shapes (one for each lizard)

Cut each egg in half using a simple wavy, curved, or zigzag line. Place three lizards in a row on the flannelboard. Let the children name the colors together. Then cover each lizard with an egg. Point to each egg and ask the children: *What color lizard is hatching from this egg?* Let the children take turns lifting up the top half of an egg to see if the correct color was named. After you repeat this activity several times, challenge the children by using four or more lizards and eggs!

Auditory Discrimination

Flannelboard activities can help young children develop the ability to recognize sounds and to hear likenesses and differences in those sounds.

Alphabet Races

Auditory discrimination

Materials: flannelboard, variety of cutouts (pattern pages 52–64)

Spread three cutouts on the floor. Let the children take turns following your oral directions for placing some of the cutouts on the flannelboard. For example: *Put the dog in the doghouse and put the cat on top of the doghouse.* After the children practice this activity, let each child have the opportunity to give oral directions.

Rhyme Time

Auditory discrimination

Materials: flannelboard; dog and chick cutouts (pattern page 53); child cutout (pattern page 58); fish cutout (pattern page 54); train cutout (pattern page 55); cat and bell cutouts (pattern page 56); mini-sentence strips; self-sticking Velcro

Add wiggly eyes to the animal cutouts. Use yarn and fabric paint to add details to the cutouts. For each cutout, print a word that rhymes with it on a separate sentence strip. Attach a "hooks" piece of Velcro to the back of each strip. Here are some rhyming word suggestions:

dog–*hog, fog, clog*
chick–*stick, kick, pick*
child–*mild, wild*
fish–*wish, dish*
train–*rain, stain, drain*
cat–*rat, bat, sat, hat, mat*
bell–*well, fell, tell*

Spread the cutouts on the floor. Place the words on the flannelboard. Point to one word and have the children say the word together. Help them think of other words that rhyme with the printed word. Challenge the children to search for a cutout from the floor with a name that rhymes with the printed word. Let the children take turns finding the cutouts and placing them next to the corresponding rhyming words on the flannelboard.

Little Larry Lizard

Auditory discrimination, alliteration, creative dramatics

Materials: flannelboard, lizard and fish cutouts (pattern page 54), elephant cutout (pattern page 52), dog cutout (pattern page 53), cat cutout (pattern page 56)

Place the cutouts randomly in a row on the flannelboard. Tell the children to listen to you as you talk about each one of the animals. After you say each alliterated sentence below, choose a child to hold up the corresponding animal from the flannelboard. Next, point to an animal on the flannelboard and help the children make up an alliterated sentence of their own. Then challenge the children to act out their sentence!

Little Larry Lizard licks lollipops.

Cute Carrie Cat catches caterpillars.

Enormous Elmo Elephant eats eggs.

Funny Fredrick Fish flops foolishly.

Dandy Donald Dog devours donuts.

What's That Sound?

Auditory discrimination

Materials: flannelboard; dog and chick cutouts (pattern page 53); airplane cutout (pattern page 54); telephone and train cutouts (pattern page 55); cat, bell, whistle, horn, and drum cutouts (pattern page 56)

Glue wiggly eyes on the animal cutouts. Use fabric paint and yarn to add other details on all the cutouts. One at a time, place a cutout on the flannelboard. Ask the children: *What sound does this make?* Let the children take turns making the sound. (For example, *Arf! Arf!* for a dog and *Wooo Wooo* for a train.) Then spread the cutouts on the floor. Make one of the sounds. Let the children take turns placing the corresponding cutout on the flannelboard.

Sounds and Pictures

Auditory discrimination, oral language

Materials: flannelboard, magazine and calendar pictures that show objects which make sounds and/or people making sounds, self-sticking Velcro

Attach a "hooks" piece of self-sticking Velcro to the back of each picture. Randomly place some of the pictures on the flannelboard. Lead the children in a discussion of what's happening in the picture and what sounds each object or person could make. Challenge the children to build a story around the picture and fill the story with sounds!

Walking Through the Tall Grass

Auditory discrimination, creative movement, oral language

Materials: flannelboard, several animal cutouts (pattern pages 52–61)

Add wiggly eyes, yarn tails, and fabric-paint details to the animal cutouts. Place the animals randomly on the flannelboard. Talk with the children about the sounds the animals make, and let the children practice making those sounds. Then teach the children the rhyme below. Tell them to pretend that they're walking through a field of tall grass out in the wilderness when suddenly they hear an animal! Let the children take turns selecting which animal they hear first, second, third, and so on for each verse. Arrange the cutouts in order on the flannelboard and have the children repeat the rhyme as you point to each animal in sequence. Let the children stand up and creatively "walk through the tall grass" to act out the verses!

Walking through the tall grass,
What do we hear?
We hear a(n) _____
Calling far and near!

" _____ !"
   (Animal sound)

Here Comes the Big Band

Auditory discrimination, creative movement

> **Materials:** flannelboard; bell, whistle, drum, horn cutouts (pattern page 56)

Use fabric paint and other decorative materials to add details to the cutouts. Place the cutouts on the flannelboard in the order that they appear in the chant below. Talk with the children about each sound the instrument makes. Let the children have fun practicing those sounds. Then teach them this rhyming chant. Let them march in place and pretend to play the instruments. As they chant each verse, point to the appropriate cutout on the flannelboard.

Here comes the big band,
Marching down the street,
*Listen to the **drum** sound,*
Wow! It's really neat!
Boom! Boom! Boom!

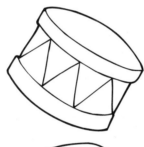

Here comes the big band,
Marching down the street,
*Listen to the **whistle** sound,*
Wow! It's really neat!
Tweet! Tweet! Tweet!

Here comes the big band,
Marching down the street,
*Listen to the **horn** sound,*
Wow! It's really neat!
Wah! Wah! Wah!

Here comes the big band,
Marching down the street,
*Listen to the **bell** sound,*
Wow! It's really neat!
Ding! Ding! Ding!

Hidden Sounds

Auditory discrimination

> **Materials:** flannelboard, large fabric rectangle, various cutouts that make sounds (pattern pages 52–64)

Place a cutout on the flannelboard and cover it up with the rectangle. Make the sound of the object, animal, or person that is hidden. Have the children take turns guessing what is making the sound. Let a child lift up the rectangle to check their guesses!

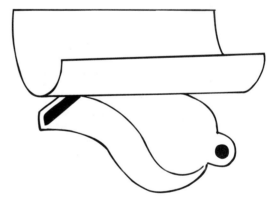

Auditory Memory

Flannelboard activities can help young children develop the ability to remember sounds after they have heard them.

Three Sounds

Auditory memory

Materials: flannelboard, variety of cutouts that make distinct sounds (pattern pages 52–64)

Randomly place three cutouts on the flannelboard. Have the children close their eyes. Tell the children to try to remember the order of the sounds you are going to make. Then make a sound that represents each one of the cutouts. For example: *Tweet! Tweet!* (whistle), *Arf! Arf!* (dog), and *Meow! Meow!* (cat). Have the children open their eyes and try to remember the order of the sounds so as to help you place the cutouts in sequence on the flannelboard. After the children do this activity several times using different cutouts, let the children take turns picking three cutouts and making the sounds for the other children to remember!

Let's Build a House

Auditory memory, color and shape recognition

Materials: flannelboard; variety of different sizes of squares, rectangles, triangles, ovals and other geometric shapes cut from solid colors of fabric

Ask the children if they would help you build a house. Spread the cutouts on the floor. Tell the children that you are going to give them a description of the house you want built. Tell them to listen carefully as you describe the house. Then give a simple description such as the following: *The house is a large blue square with a red triangle roof. It has two green square windows and a green rectangle door.* Challenge the children to help you "build" the house from memory! Help the children remember by asking key questions: *What color is the house? What is its shape? What color roof does it have? How many windows? What color are the windows? What shape are the windows? Does it have a door? What color is the door? What shape is the door?* Let the children take turns helping you find the correct shapes.

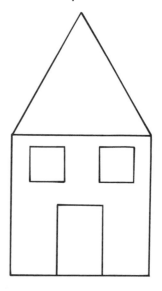

Circus Time

Auditory memory, color recognition

Materials: flannelboard, several animal cutouts (pattern pages 52–61), five circus stand cutouts in different colors (pattern page 57)

Add wiggly eyes on the animals. Use fabric paint to add facial and body features. Use fabric paint to add zigzag designs on the circus stands.

Randomly place three circus stands on the flannelboard. Tell the children that you need their help in arranging the animals in the circus. Spread the animal cutouts on the floor. Give three directions for placing certain animals on specific circus stands. For example: *Put the elephant on the red stand. Put the dog on the green stand. Put the cat on the yellow stand.* Then select a child to follow the oral directions you have given. Challenge the children by using more than three circus stands. As a follow-up activity, teach the children the following rhyme. Let them pretend to be clowns and act out the rhyme as they recite it.

Circus time has come to town!
Look at me! I am a clown!
Both my feet are very BIG,
I can dance and do a jig!

Let's Go Fly a Kite!

Auditory memory

Materials: flannelboard, several fabric diamond shapes

Make each diamond shape into a kite by adding a thin yarn tail. Spread out three kites on the floor. Tell the children to listen carefully as you explain how to arrange the kites on the flannelboard. Then give the children directions such as these: *Place the green-striped kite in the middle. Place the blue-dotted kite last. Put the orange kite first.* Then select a child to follow your directions from memory. Let other children try this with new directions. Challenge the children by having them arrange more than three kites on the flannelboard!

Stars in the Night Sky

Auditory memory, color recognition

Materials: flannelboard, several star cutouts in a variety of solid colors (pattern page 57)

Randomly place the stars on the flannelboard. Tell the children that you are going to say a rhyme and name three different color stars. Challenge the children to remember which color stars you name. Have the children close their eyes while you recite the following rhyme. Name a color star for each blank in the rhyme. After the rhyme, have a volunteer remove the appropriate stars from the flannelboard.

Stars in the night sky,
Stars blinking up high,
Which starlight,
Will I wish on tonight?
The _____ star,
The _____ star,
And the _____ star.

Birthday Presents

Auditory memory, color recognition

Materials: flannelboard, several cutouts (pattern pages 52–64), several large squares of colorful fabric (one for each cutout), gift bows, self-sticking Velcro

Randomly place two cutouts on the flannelboard. Spread out the squares of fabric on the floor. Attach a "hooks" piece of Velcro to the back of each bow. Place the bows on the floor. Tell the children you need them to help you "wrap the birthday presents" on the flannelboard. Then give the children simple wrapping instructions for each cutout. For example, *Wrap the dog with the blue box. Wrap the cat with the red box.* Let the children take turns placing the squares over the appropriate cutouts. Then give the children directions for placing the bows on the presents. For example, *Place the blue bow on the red box. Place the white bow on the blue box.* Let the children take turns placing the bows on the boxes. After the children practice this activity, have them wrap three presents from memory!

Ten Silly Roosters

Identifying and creating a pattern

> **Materials:** flannelboard, 10 rooster cutouts (pattern page 57), brown fabric strips

Arrange the brown fabric strips to create a fence across the flannelboard. Use fabric paint, wiggly eyes, and yarn to add details to the roosters. Place the roosters on top of the fence in a row. Tell the children to close their eyes and listen carefully to your story. Then recite the story rhyme below. Choose a number between *1* and *10* to represent the blank in the third line. Have the children open their eyes. Select a volunteer to rely on his or her memory to remove the number of roosters you recited in the rhyme.

Ten silly roosters,
Lined up in a row,
_____ flew away,
When they all began to crow—
Cock-a-doodle-doo!

Brain Game

Auditory memory, creating a pattern

> **Materials:** flannelboard; four each of small geometric fabric shapes—square, rectangle, triangle, oval—in a variety of solid colors (make each geometric shape the same color and different from the other shapes)

Tell the children that you are going to teach them the "Brain Game." Spread out all the shapes on the floor. Have the children close their eyes while you say aloud a pattern of shapes. For example, *Square, square, triangle, oval, square, square, triangle, oval.* Let the children open their eyes and take turns creating the pattern from memory on the flannelboard.

Meanings of Position Words

Flannelboard activities can help reinforce the meanings of position words—in, out, over, under, top, bottom, and more!

Dog on the Doghouse

Position words, auditory memory

Materials: flannelboard, dog cutout (one for each child) and doghouse cutout (pattern page 53)

Glue wiggly eyes on the dogs. Add other details with fabric paint and yarn. Give each child a dog cutout. Place the doghouse on the flannelboard. Using a position word, instruct each child to place his or her dog on the flannelboard in relation to the doghouse. Provide a specific instruction to each child. For example, *Lauren, put your dog under the doghouse. Ramon, put your dog in the doghouse.* Let each child place his or her dog on the flannelboard.

Trucking

Position words

Materials: flannelboard, long narrow strips of fabric, truck cutout (pattern page 59), one red square and one green square

Place the fabric strips on the flannelboard so that they intersect and parallel one another to resemble streets. Place the green square at one end of the "maze" of streets and the red square at the other end. Tell the children you need their help in getting the truck from the green "go" square to the red "stop" square. Let a child move the truck through the maze as you give step-by-step directions. Use words such as *left, right, up,* and *down* in your directions. For example, *Move the truck up one block and to the right another block.* When the truck reaches the red square, have all the children shout "Stop!" Repeat with other children "at the wheel!"

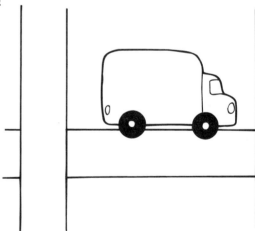

Sailing, Sailing

Position words, opposites

Materials: flannelboard, fabric cut into the shape of a sailboat, blue fabric cut in the shape of a lake, fabric tree

Place the tree on the flannelboard. Place the lake near the tree. Let the children take turns manipulating the sailboat on the flannelboard according to your statements. (For example: *The sailboat is **in** the water. The sailboat is **out** of the water. The sailboat is on **top** of the tree. The sailboat is on the **bottom** of the tree. The sailboat is **behind** the tree. The sailboat is in **front** of the tree.*) For each pair of statements, use word opposites. Emphasize these words so the children begin to understand the meanings of word opposites.

Load Up the Wagon

Position words

Materials: flannelboard, several small cutouts (one for each child; pattern pages 52–64), enlarged wagon cutout (pattern page 59)

Use wiggly eyes, yarn, and fabric paint to add details to the cutouts. Give each child a cutout. Place the wagon on the flannelboard. Tell the children they are going to load the wagon with their cutouts. Call on each child to place his or her cutout *in, under, near, above,* or *beside* the wagon. Then return the cutouts and let the children take turns placing them on the flannelboard. Have the rest of the children tell where each cutout was placed. For example, *Mary put her bear **in** the wagon.*

A Flannelboard Zoo

Position words, oral language, vocabulary

Materials: flannelboard; lion, camel, hippo, and giraffe cutouts (pattern page 60); elephant and bear cutouts (pattern page 52); lizard cutout (pattern page 54); various pieces of fabric cut into these shapes: a hill, a pond, a tree, a large rock, a tuft of grass

Use wiggly eyes, yarn, and fabric paint to add details to the cutout animals. Then set up a "zoo" on the flannelboard using all the cutouts. First, place the hill, the pond, the tree, the rock, and the grass on the flannelboard. Next, put the different cutouts on the flannelboard in relation to the environment you created. Tell the children that they are going to visit a flannelboard zoo. Let the children have fun talking about the zoo. Encourage the children to use sentences such as the following: *I see a giraffe near the water. I see a lizard in the grass.* Ask the children these kinds of questions: *What animal is **in** the tree? What animal is **behind** the rock?* After awhile, let the children reposition the animals and tell where they are placing the animals. Encourage the children to use position words.

Acorns for the Squirrel

Position words, auditory memory

Materials: flannelboard, squirrel and several acorn cutouts (one for each child; pattern page 61), fabric tree

Use wiggly eyes and fabric paint to add details to the squirrel. Put the fabric tree and the squirrel on the flannelboard. Scatter the acorns on the floor and say to the children: *I'm going to tell you where to put the acorns. Listen to my direction.* Then give the children a simple direction such as *Put an acorn **in** the tree* or *Put an acorn **under** the squirrel.* Let the children take turns placing an acorn on the flannelboard according to each direction you give. With practice, the children will want to be giving the directions for the other children to follow!

A Mouse House

Position words

Materials: flannelboard; large fabric rectangle for the house; large fabric triangle for the roof; mouse cutout (pattern page 59); magazine pictures of household items: kitchen pots and pans, bed, sofa, bathtub, dining table; five small fabric rectangles; self-sticking Velcro; tagboard

Use wiggly eyes, yarn, and fabric paint to add details to the mouse. Glue a piece of tagboard to the back of each magazine picture. Then trim each picture so it forms a cutout. Attach a "hooks" piece of Velcro to the back of each magazine cutout. Put the "mouse house" on the flannelboard. Place the magazine cutouts within the house to create the illusion of different rooms—kitchen, living room, bedroom, bathroom. Stack the five rectangles to form a set of stairs. Then use sentences with position words to let the children manipulate the mouse in and around the house. For example, *Have the mouse go **up** the stairs. Have the mouse go **down** the stairs. Put the mouse **under** the rug. Put the mouse **on** the sofa.* As a follow-up activity, let the children take turns manipulating the mouse on the flannelboard as they tell a story about the mouse in the house.

Table Talk

Position words, oral language

Materials: flannelboard, fabric rectangle, four fabric strips, various cutouts (pattern pages 52–64)

Use wiggly eyes, yarn, and fabric paint to add details to the cutouts. Form a table on the flannelboard using the rectangle for the tabletop and the four strips for the legs. Spread the cutouts on the floor. Let the children take turns choosing a cutout to place on the flannelboard table. Have each child describe where he or she is putting the cutout. For example, *I am putting the dog on top of the table.*

Identifying Letters

These flannelboard activities will give the children practice in identifying letters that look alike.

Find the Letters

Identifying letters

Materials: flannelboard, two sets of uppercase alphabet cutouts, 12 fabric circles (big enough to cover an alphabet letter)

Arrange two sets of six letters on the flannelboard in four rows, three letters in each row. Cover each letter with a fabric circle. Tell the children to try to find the matching letters. Let the children take turns lifting pairs of circles to find matching letters. If the letters match, remove the circles. If a match isn't found, replace the circles. Repeat this activity several times using different letters.

Alphabet Train

Identifying letters, oral language

Materials: flannelboard, uppercase and lowercase letter cutouts, train engine cutout and several train car cutouts (pattern page 55)

Use fabric paint to add details to the train. Add wheels on the train with fabric circles and brass fasteners. Place the train on the flannelboard. On the engine and on each train car, place an uppercase letter. Spread out the lowercase letters on the floor. While the children recite the rhyme below, let another child find the matching lowercase letters from the floor and place each one next to its match on the train. Repeat the activity using different letters.

See the train move along the track,
With a chug, chug, choo, choo, choo!
Hear the rails go clickety-clack,
With a chug, chug, choo, choo, choo!

Wooo! Wooo! Wooo!

Look Around

Identifying letters, oral language

Materials: flannelboard, uppercase and lowercase letters, various cutouts that begin with different letters of the alphabet (pattern pages 52–64)

Use wiggly eyes, yarn, and fabric paint to add details to the cutouts. Place one cutout on the flannelboard. Have the children say the name of the cutout. Ask the children: *What is the beginning letter sound?* Let the children help you find the uppercase and lowercase letters and place them on the flannelboard next to the cutout. (For example: *L* and *l* are placed next to a lion cutout.) Repeat this activity again and again. Teach the children the rhyme below. Let the children take turns finding the letters appropriate for each cutout while the rest of the children recite the rhyme. Replace the blanks in the first line with the name of the child looking for the letters. See how far the children count before the letters are found!

_____, _____, (child's name)
Look around,
Find the letters,
On the ground!

_____, _____, (child's name)
Look with glee,
Hear us counting,
One, two, three, . . .

Match Up

Identifying letters

Materials: flannelboard, uppercase and lowercase letters

Give each child one or more uppercase letters. Place the lowercase letters in rows alphabetically on the flannelboard, leaving space between each letter. Let the children take turns placing their letters next to the matching lowercase letters on the flannelboard. Repeat the activity. This time give the children the lowercase letters and place the uppercase letters in rows on the flannelboard.

Word-Picture Association

Flannelboard activities help the children develop their ability to associate words and pictures about home safety, fire safety, plant life, and more.

Home Safety

Word-picture association, safety

Materials: flannelboard; first-aid kit, poison bottle, bandage, and medicine bottle cutouts (pattern page 63); telephone cutout (pattern page 55); child and adult cutouts (pattern page 58); *911* number cutouts

Use fabric paint to add details to the cutouts. Randomly place the cutouts on the flannelboard. Hold up the child and adult cutouts. Tell a simple story about what this child should do if he or she gets hurt. Talk about the poison symbol on bottles, how only parents or adults should give medicine, and how to use the telephone in emergencies.

Stop! Drop! Roll!

Word-picture association, fire safety

Materials: flannelboard; match and fire extinguisher cutouts (pattern page 61); child and adult cutouts (pattern page 58); gray fabric cut in the shape of billowing smoke; orange or red fabric cut in the shape of flames; *911* number cutouts

Use fabric paint to add details to the cutouts. Spread the cutouts on the floor. Talk about fire safety. Put the people cutouts on the flannelboard. As you place each of the other cutouts on the flannelboard, talk about its importance. Tell the children that if their clothes or hair catches on fire, they should follow these directions: *Stop! Drop to the floor! Roll to put out the fire!* Talk about the purpose of the *911* emergency telephone number. After you talk about the meaning of each of the cutouts, let the children take turns manipulating the cutouts to tell something about fire safety.

Safety Walk

Word-picture association, safety

Materials: flannelboard, six traffic sign cutouts (pattern page 62)

Use fabric paint to add details to the cutouts. Randomly place the traffic sign cutouts on the flannelboard. Talk about the meaning of each sign. Then let the children take turns manipulating the child cutout as you guide the children in a language experience story about a child walking down the sidewalk and seeing each street sign.

Vroom! Vroom!

Word-picture association, introduce traffic signs

Materials: flannelboard, six traffic sign cutouts (pattern page 62)

Use fabric paint to add details to the traffic signs. Tell the children to pretend they are driving cars. Guide the children through this activity by giving directions such as the following:

> Take out your keys. Unlock the driver's door. Get in the driver's seat. Adjust your mirrors. Put the key in the starter and turn the key. Vroom! Vroom! goes the engine. Look in your mirror to see that there are no cars, trucks, buses, or people in your way. Put on your turn signal and turn onto the street. Here we go!

Let the children "drive their cars" a little while, and then put up a traffic sign on the flannelboard. Have the children stop their cars and notice the sign. Talk about the sign and what it means. As the children become more and more familiar with these signs, let them take turns telling you what each sign means!

Picture-Word Fun

Word-picture association

Materials: flannelboard, various cutouts (pattern pages 52–64), mini-sentence strips, self-sticking Velcro

Position each sentence strip vertically. Tape a cutout to the top half of the strip and write the name of the cutout on the bottom half. Cut each strip in half with a simple pattern so the halves can be easily matched. Attach a "hooks" piece of Velcro to the back of each half. Place the pictures on the flannelboard. Spread out the words on the floor. Let the children take turns matching the pictures and words. After the matches are made, read the words together.

Growing Plants

Word-picture association, plants

Materials: flannelboard, sun cutout (pattern page 59), blue fabric cut into raindrop shapes, black fabric cut into seed shapes, green fabric cut into the shapes of a stem and leaves, brown fabric cut into wavy strips for plant roots, yellow fabric cut into the shape of a flower, strip of brown fabric for the soil, mini-sentence strips, self-sticking Velcro

Write the name of each plant part—*flower, stem, leaf, roots, seed*—on a separate sentence strip. Beside each name draw a simple picture symbol of the part. Attach a "hooks" piece of self-sticking Velcro to the back of each sentence strip. Place the strips on the flannelboard. Talk with the children about what is needed to grow plants—seeds, soil, sun, and water. Place the corresponding shapes on the flannelboard. Then tell the children the different parts of a plant and place each cutout on the flannelboard as you describe it. Move the label next to its matching plant part. When the children understand the different plant parts and can "read" the labels, mix up the labels and plant parts. Challenge the children to find the matches!

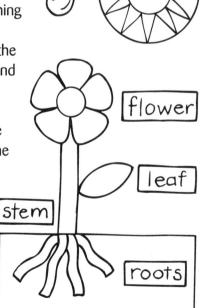

Healthy Habits

Word-picture association, health

Materials: flannelboard; magazine pictures showing child practicing healthy habits—brushing teeth, sleeping, running, brushing hair, eating healthy foods, bathing; tagboard; self-sticking Velcro; mini-sentence strips

Glue each picture to tagboard and attach a "hooks" piece of Velcro to the back of each picture. Write simple healthy habits on separate sentence strips: *Brush teeth. Brush hair. Wash. Eat good food. Sleep. Exercise.* Attach a "hooks" piece of Velcro to the back of each strip.

Place the sentence strips in a vertical column on the flannelboard. Talk about each one with the children. Spread out the pictures on the floor. Let the children take turns matching the pictures with the good health habit labels. Mix up the labels and pictures. Let the children help you match them up correctly once again!

Weather Symbols

Word-picture association, weather

Materials: flannelboard, five mini-sentence strips, self-sticking Velcro

Cut the sentence strips in half to create cards. Write the name of a kind of weather—*snowy, cloudy, rainy, windy, sunny*—on separate cards and draw a simple weather symbol beside each name. Make two sets of these cards. Attach a "hooks" piece of Velcro above the weather word on each card. Hold up each card and talk with the children about each kind of weather. Then place the 10 cards in rows on the flannelboard so that the pictures and words are facing the flannelboard. Let the children take turns turning over two cards at a time to see if they match. If they match, say aloud the kind of weather printed on the cards and place the cards on the floor. If the cards don't match, return them to their positions on the flannelboard.

Letter-Sound Recognition

These flannelboard activities will give the children practice in recognizing the sounds of letters.

What's That Sound?

Letter-sound recognition

Materials: flannelboard, alphabet cutouts, large fabric square

Place an uppercase letter and its matching lowercase letter on the flannelboard. Cover them with the fabric square. Tell the children to try to discover what letters are hidden under the square. Say the sound the letters make. Let the children guess which letter makes that sound. Have each guesser take a peek under the square to see if his or her guess is correct. Repeat with other sets of letters.

Letter-Picture Puzzles

Letter-sound recognition

Materials: flannelboard, mini-sentence strips, pictures cut from magazines or old calendars, self-sticking Velcro

To create the letter-picture puzzles, cut each sentence strip in half using a variety of simple wavy, zigzag, and curved lines. Print an uppercase letter on one half of a sentence strip. Cut out a simple picture whose name begins with that letter and glue it on the matching half of the strip. Attach a "hooks" piece of Velcro to the back of each half.

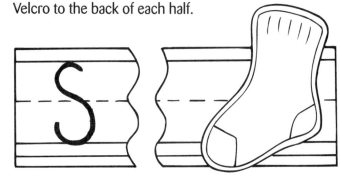

Spread out the picture puzzle halves on the floor. Place one of the letter halves on the flannelboard. Say its name and have the children repeat its name with you. Say the sound of the letter and have the children repeat the sound. Encourage the children to think of words beginning with that sound. Let the children take turns finding the matching picture half and placing it on the flannelboard to complete the puzzle.

Teacher Says

Letter-sound recognition

Materials: flannelboard, alphabet cutouts

Match the uppercase and lowercase letters and place them in order on the flannelboard. Tell the children they are going to play "Teacher Says." Have the children repeat whatever you say **only** if you first say *Teacher says!* Tell the children that if you don't say *Teacher says,* they are to say nothing! Point to each letter of the alphabet and say *Teacher says;* then say its name and repeat the sound it makes three times. For example, *Teacher says* **bee**—*beh, beh, beh.* Remember to leave off *Teacher says* sometimes to make the game fun!

Sound Express

Letter-sound recognition

Materials: flannelboard, uppercase letter cutouts, train cutouts (pattern page 55)

Use fabric paint to add details to the train cutouts. Place the train on the flannelboard. Spread out the letters on the floor. Tell the children that the train is called the Sound Express and carries letters of the alphabet. Let the children discover which letters the train is carrying. Make the sounds of three different letters. For example: *Ah, Beh, Fff.* Then let the children try to find the letters that make those sounds and place them on the train. Repeat this activity several times. Challenge the children to take turns making a letter sound and having the rest of the children find the matching letter to place on the train!

Word Completion

Flannelboard activities give young children practice in finding missing letters from partial words, an important readiness skill that leads to reading words.

Find the Letters

Word completion

Materials: flannelboard, two sets of alphabet cutouts

Use the alphabet cutouts to spell out a column of simple words on the flannelboard. Next to each word, place one letter from the word. Spread out the rest of the alphabet cutouts on the floor. Let the children take turns finding the missing letters and completing each word. Say the word together as it's completed.

Complete the Word

Word completion

Materials: flannelboard; variety of cutouts with simple names such as the cat, bell, drum, and horn cutouts (pattern page 56; one for each child); mini-sentence strips; self-sticking Velcro; alphabet cutouts

Use fabric paint, yarn, and wiggly eyes to add details to the cutouts. Write the name of each cutout on a separate sentence strip. Attach a "hooks" piece of Velcro to the back of each strip. Spread the letter cutouts on the floor. Place a word strip and its matching cutout on the flannelboard. Have the children say the word with you. Using the alphabet letters, place two letters from the name of the cutout on the flannelboard. Let the children take turns completing the word by finding the missing alphabet cutouts from the floor and placing them correctly on the flannelboard.

Missing Letters

Word completion

Materials: flannelboard, mini-sentence strips, self-sticking Velcro, alphabet cutouts

Print simple words, such as *cat, dog, zoo, boy, girl, car,* and *hat,* on separate sentence strips. Cut the sentence strips in half, if needed. Attach a "hooks" piece of Velcro to the back of each strip. Place the strips in a vertical row on the flannelboard. Next to each strip, spell out the word using the alphabet cutouts. Remove one letter cutout from each word and place the cutout on the floor. Let the children take turns completing the words by finding the missing letters from the floor. Challenge the children to read aloud each word as it is completed!

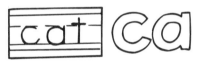 

Story Time

Word completion

Materials: flannelboard, two sets of alphabet cutouts

Tell a simple story such as the one below. When you come to an easy word such as c*at, dog, rat,* or *sun,* spell out the word on the flannelboard using the alphabet cutouts. You may also want to use cutouts (pattern pages 52–64) to help tell a story.

> *A cat met a rat. They played and played in the sun. They got so tired that they fell asleep. Along came a dog. Sniff! Sniff! went the dog. The cat and rat woke up. The dog barked! He wanted to play. But the cat and rat were still too sleepy so the three friends slept all day. Then they woke up and played!*

After you tell the story, point to each word you spelled out on the flannelboard and have the children say the word with you. Below each word, place two letters from the word. Let the children take turns completing the words.

Sight-Word Recognition

Help young children recognize frequently used words with these flannelboard activities.

Dog Bones

Listening

Materials: flannelboard, 3 different-colored dog cutouts and 10 bone cutouts (pattern page 53)

Use fabric paint and wiggly eyes to add details to the dog cutouts. Make a list of 10 frequently used words that the children hear and see in their reading. Write each one on a bone cutout using a nontoxic permanent marker. Choose three words at a time for this activity. Place the dogs and dog bones on the flannelboard. Point to each word and say it aloud. Have the children repeat the word with you. Then challenge the children to match certain words with specific dogs. For example: *Put **jump** by the brown dog.*

Helping Mr. Squirrel

Sight-word recognition

Materials: flannelboard, 1 squirrel cutout and 10 acorn cutouts (pattern page 61), strip of green fabric as long as the flannelboard

Use fabric paint and wiggly eyes to add details to the squirrel. Cut slits along one side of the green strip to represent grass and place the grass along the bottom of the flannelboard. Make a list of 10 frequently used words that the children see in their reading. Write one of these words on each acorn cutout using a nontoxic permanent marker. Choose four words at a time for this activity. Hold up each acorn and read aloud the word. Have the children repeat the word with you. Then tuck the acorns under the grass on the flannelboard. Tell the children that Mr. Squirrel needs their help in finding two very special acorns. Choose two words for the children to find. Say the words one at a time. Let the children take turns putting Mr. Squirrel on the flannelboard and searching through the grass to find the acorn with the correct word. As each word is found, have the children say it and place the acorn on top of the grass.

Under the Tent

Sight-word recognition

Materials: flannelboard, three large fabric triangles, mini-sentence strips, self-sticking Velcro

Make a tent out of each triangle by drawing a line down the middle from the highest point to the middle point on the bottom of the triangle. Cut a slit along that line, leaving the triangle connected at the top. Print 12 frequently used words on sentence strips. Attach a "hooks" piece of Velcro to the back of each strip.

Place the tents on the flannelboard. Hide a word strip behind each tent. Invite a child to lift a flap on a tent and pull out the word strip. Let the child or another classmate read the word aloud. After each word is read, let the child replace the word behind the tent. Challenge the children to remember which word is behind each tent. Say to the children: *Under which tent is the word **girl**?* Repeat this activity using different words. When the children are able to easily recognize each word, let them take turns hiding words under the tents!

Mail Call!

Sight-word recognition, shape and color recognition

Materials: flannelboard, variety of simple geometric shapes in different colors, small letter-size envelopes, self-sticking Velcro

Print a set of frequently used words on the backs of separate envelopes. Attach a "hooks" piece of Velcro to the front of each envelope and place the envelopes on the flannelboard. Spread out the geometric shapes on the floor. Point to each word on an envelope and have the children say the word aloud. Challenge the children to place certain shapes inside specific envelopes by giving them directions such as the following: *Put a green triangle inside the **hat** envelope. Put a red circle inside the **pet** envelope.* Let the children take turns finding the shapes and placing them in the appropriate envelopes. This fun activity will give the children lots of practice in reading sight words as well as in recognizing colors and shapes!

Sequencing and Tracking

Use these activities to help young children develop their ability to order objects and events and to track from left to right.

Step by Step

Sequencing events, oral language, tracking

Materials: flannelboard, sets of four pictures showing step-by-step ways to do things such as brushing teeth and making a sandwich (old workbooks are good resources), self-sticking Velcro

Attach a "hooks" piece of Velcro to the back of each picture. Randomly place a set of pictures on the flannelboard. Talk with the children about each step they would take to do the activity. Let the children take turns placing the pictures in order. Review each activity by saying each step and letting different children point to the pictures, tracking from left to right.

Art Time

Sequencing events, listening, creative dramatics

Materials: flannelboard; pencil, glue bottle, and scissors cutouts (pattern page 64); crayon cutout (pattern page 52); white fabric rectangle

Use fabric paint to add details to the cutouts. Spread the cutouts on the floor. Tell the children you are going to tell them how to do an imaginary art project. Have the children listen carefully as you explain each step. Let the children take turns manipulating the cutouts in order on the flannelboard and dramatizing each action. Say to the children: *First, get a pencil and a sheet of paper. Next, draw a picture on the paper. Color the picture with a crayon. Then cut out the picture with scissors. Finally, take a glue bottle and glue the picture on the flannelboard!* Let the children practice this activity several times; each time order the steps a bit differently.

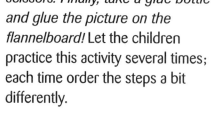

Planting Flowers

Sequencing events

Materials: flannelboard, clay pot and flower cutouts (pattern page 64), blue fabric cut into a raindrop shape, black fabric cut into seed shapes, green fabric strip for the stem, sun cutout (pattern page 59), light brown fabric oval to use for the soil

Use fabric paint to add details to the cutouts. Tell the children each step in growing a flower: (1) put good soil in a pot, (2) plant seeds in the soil, (3) water the seeds, (4) let the sun warm the seeds, and (5) watch the flower grow! As you say each step, place the necessary cutouts in sequence on the flannelboard. Say the steps again letting the children take turns manipulating the cutouts in sequence.

The Train Ride

Sequencing animals, tracking

Materials: flannelboard, variety of animal cutouts (pattern pages 52–61), train cutouts (pattern page 55)

Use wiggly eyes, yarn, and fabric paint to add details to the cutouts. Place the train on the flannelboard. Spread the animal cutouts on the floor. Decide which animal will be picked up first, second, third, and so on, by the train. Teach the children the rhyme below. As you recite the rhyme and "move" the train on the flannelboard, let the children take turns placing the animal cutouts in sequence on the train.

The little train went down the track,
Carrying critters on its back,
Wooo! Wooo! Choo! Choo!
Clickety, clickety, clack!

The little train soon stopped to say,
"I'll pick up this _____ on my way!"
Wooo! Wooo! Choo! Choo!
Clickety, clickety, clack!

The little train soon stopped to say,
"I'll pick up this _____ on my way!"
Wooo! Wooo! Choo! Choo! (and so on)

We-Have-Fun Photos

Sequencing events, oral language

Materials: flannelboard; a sequence of classroom photographs of daily, routine activities; mini-sentence strips; self-sticking Velcro

Attach a "hooks" piece of Velcro to the back of each photograph. Print a caption for each photograph on separate sentence strips. (For example, *Reading Time, Play Time, Story Time, Art Table,* etc.) Attach a "hooks" piece of Velcro to the back of each caption. Talk with the children about their school day and which activities they enjoy. Show the children each picture, and let them describe what is happening in the photograph. Place the photograph and its caption on the flannelboard. Then let the children help you sequence the activities chronologically from left to right on the flannelboard.

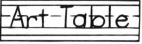

Hatching Baby Chicks

Sequencing events, tracking

Materials: flannelboard, two chick cutouts (pattern page 53), four hen cutouts (pattern page 57), two white pieces of fabric shaped like chicken eggs, white pieces of fabric shaped like "hatched eggs" (cut in half with zigzag lines), thin strips of brown fabric to make the chicken nests

Arrange the cutouts on the flannelboard from left to right to show a sequence of four events: *hen next to its nest, hen resting on its nest, hen resting on a nest of eggs,* and *broken "hatched" eggs with two baby chicks next to mother hen.* Then tell the children the order of events. Let the children take turns pointing to each set of cutouts. Try mixing up the events on the flannelboard and letting the children help you reorder them.

The Melting Snowman

Sequencing events, oral language, tracking

Materials: flannelboard, sun cutout (pattern page 59), one small white fabric circle, two medium-size white fabric circles, three large fabric circles, four top hats cut out of black fabric, three different-sized "puddle of water" shapes cut out of light blue fabric

If you want, use fabric paint to make a face on the snowman's head (small white fabric circle). Arrange the cutouts on the flannelboard from left to right to show the following sequence:

- *Stack three circles of varying sizes to form a snowman. Place the top hat on its head.*

- *Put the sun above the "melting snowman." Make the melting snowman by placing one medium-size circle on top of one large circle and place the two circles on a puddle of water shape. Put the top hat on the water shape.*

- *Put the sun above the "melting snowman." Make the melting snowman by placing just one large circle on a puddle of water shape. Put the top hat on the water shape.*

- *Put the top hat on a puddle of water shape and place the sun above the hat.*

Let the children tell you what is happening in each picture. As you retell the events, let the children take turns tracking the events from left to right by using their fingers or a pointer.

Cleanup Time

Sequencing objects, oral language

Materials: flannelboard; cat, bell, whistle, drum, and horn cutouts (pattern page 56); boy and girl child cutouts (pattern page 58); wagon cutout (pattern page 59)

Use fabric paint to add details to the cutouts. Place the girl, the boy, and the wagon cutouts on the flannelboard. Place the rest of the cutouts along the bottom of the flannelboard. Tell the children to help the boy and girl "clean up" their toys by deciding which order to put the toys in the wagon. Let the children take turns sequencing the toys on the flannelboard. After a child has ordered the toys, let another child put each toy in order in the wagon. Have the child name each toy he or she is placing in the wagon.

Listening and Responding to a Story

Help young children develop their ability to listen to stories and respond to them using these flannelboard activities.

Cock-a-doodle Do!

Listening, responding to a story, oral language

Materials: flannelboard, rooster cutout (pattern page 57), dog and chick cutouts (pattern page 53), cat cutout (pattern page 56), mouse cutout (pattern page 59), a variety of other farm animal cutouts made from coloring books

Use wiggly eyes, yarn, and fabric paint to add details to the cutouts. (If you use paper cutouts from coloring books, attach a "hooks" piece of self-sticking Velcro to the back of each cutout.) Place the rooster on the flannelboard. Spread out the remaining farm animal cutouts on the floor. Begin the story rhyme below. Let the children take turns finding the corresponding animal for each verse and placing it on the flannelboard. When the words *Let's run and run and run* are spoken, have the child who is placing the animal on the flannelboard make the rooster and the animal "run and run and run." Children will easily learn this story rhyme so encourage their oral participation.

There was a little rooster,
Who got up with the sun,
"Cock-a-doodle-doo!" said he,
"It's time to have some fun!"

The rooster woke the animals,
He called them one by one,
"Wake up, Cat! Wake up, Cat!
"Let's run and run and run!"

The rooster woke the animals,
He called them one by one,
"Wake up, Chick! Wake up, Chick!
"Let's run and run and run!"

The rooster woke the animals,
He called them one by one,
"Wake up, Dog! Wake up, Dog!
"Let's run and run and run!"

The rooster woke the animals,
He called them one by one,
"Wake up, Mouse! Wake up, Mouse!
"Let's run and run and run!"

(Add additional verses if you have more cutouts.)

A Cat and Mouse Fable

Listening, responding to a story

Materials: flannelboard, cat and bell cutouts (pattern page 56), several mouse cutouts (pattern page 59)

Use fabric paint and wiggly eyes to add details to the cutouts. Let the children listen to you tell the following fable. Manipulate the cutouts as you tell the tale.

Once upon a time, some mice lived in a big house. The mice loved the big house. Bits of cheese fell from the table. Cracker crumbs fell from the table. Bread crumbs fell from the table. Water dripped from the faucet. All night long the mice scurried and scampered eating and drinking. "What a feast!" said the biggest mouse. Then he puffed out his chest.

*One night they heard a scary sound—**MEOW!** "What was that?" asked the tiniest mouse.*

"A cat!" whispered the biggest mouse.

"What's a cat?" squeaked the tiniest mouse.

"Wait and see," warned the biggest mouse. Then he puffed out his chest. All night long the mice scurried and scampered eating and drinking. Suddenly the cat pounced! "MEOW!"

The mice ran. The cat ran. They ran and ran. The mice ran inside their mouse hole. "We must stop this cat from scaring us!" said the biggest mouse. Then he puffed out his chest. "I have a plan, he said. "While the cat is sleeping, let's tie a bell on its collar. Then we can hear the bell ring when the cat is coming!"

"Hooray!" shouted the mice. "Hooray for the biggest mouse!" The biggest mouse puffed out his chest even more.

"But who will tie the bell on the cat?" asked the tiniest mouse. No one said a word. All the mice looked at the biggest mouse. But he didn't speak. He just stopped puffing out his chest.

After the story, talk with the children about its lesson: *Even the best plan isn't good if no one will do it.* Ask the children these kinds of questions: *Why do you think the tiniest mouse didn't know what a cat was? How do you think the mice felt when the cat pounced? What might happen if you wanted healthy teeth but you didn't follow a plan for healthy teeth by brushing your teeth every day?* You might even tell the story again and let the children take turns helping you manipulate the cutouts on the flannelboard.

The Lion and the Mouse

Listening, responding to a story, oral language

Materials: flannelboard, lion cutout (pattern page 60), mouse cutout (pattern page 59), piece of netting, self-sticking Velcro

Use wiggly eyes, yarn, and fabric paint to add details to the cutouts. Attach a "hooks" piece of self-sticking Velcro to the back of the netting. As you tell the fable below, manipulate the cutouts on the flannelboard.

Once upon a time, a lion was sleeping in a jungle. A mouse crawled over him and began chewing on the lion's tail. The lion woke up! "Roar!" shouted the lion. "What a fine breakfast you will make!"

"Oh, please, Lion," pleaded the mouse. "Let me go. I shall never forget your kindness. I promise to help you if you need me."

"Ha! Ha!" laughed the lion. "A little mouse like you helping the King of the Jungle like me? How can that be?" But the mouse pleaded and pleaded and the lion decided to let the mouse go.

The very next day the mouse heard the lion's roar. The mouse ran toward the sound and saw the lion caught in a hunter's net. "I'll help you," said the mouse.

"Ha! Ha!" laughed the lion. "A little mouse like you helping the King of the Jungle like me? How can that be?" But the mouse chewed and chewed the net and set the lion free. "You may be little," said the lion to the mouse, "but you are a great friend!"

After the story ask the children these kinds of questions: *Do you think the mouse is brave? Do you think the lion is really the King of the Jungle? Why? Do you think the mouse is really a "great friend" to the lion? Why? If your friend needed help, how could you help him or her?* Then tell the story again, and let the children take turns manipulating the cutouts on the flannelboard.

Ring! Ring! Ring!

Listening, responding to a story, oral language

Materials: flannelboard, two telephone cutouts (pattern page 55), number cutouts

Use fabric paint to print *0, 1, 2, 3, 4, 5, 6, 7, 8, 9* and other details on the telephone cutouts. Let each child have a turn using the number cutouts to display his or her phone number on the flannelboard. Place the two telephones on the flannelboard and let two children at a time go to the flannelboard. Have one child "call home" on one telephone and the other child act as Mom or Dad answering the telephone. Have the rest of the children sing the song below to the tune of "Are You Sleeping?"

I am dialing,
I am dialing,
On the phone,
On the phone,
Pushing on the numbers,
Pushing on the numbers,
Ring, ring, ring,
Ring, ring, ring!

Hello, Mother (Father),
Hello, Mother (Father),
How are you?
How are you?
Calling you is such fun,
So long now, I must run,
Bye, bye, bye,
Bye, bye, bye!

Hello, _____, (child's name)
Hello, _____, (child's name)
How are you?
How are you?
Hearing you is such fun,
So long now, I must run,
Bye, bye, bye,
Bye, bye, bye!

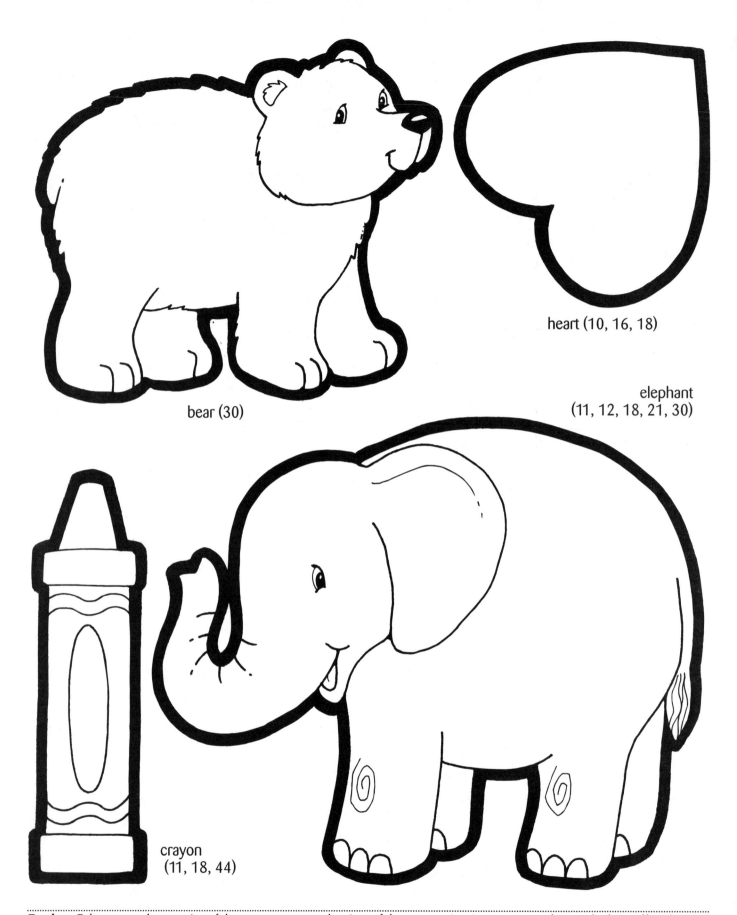

bear (30)

heart (10, 16, 18)

elephant
(11, 12, 18, 21, 30)

crayon
(11, 18, 44)

Teacher: Enlarge or reduce copies of the patterns to vary the sizes of the cutouts. Laminate or cover them with clear self-sticking paper for sturdiness. Use them as cutouts or as templates for tracing on felt or other fabrics.

chick (13, 18, 20, 21, 46, 48)

dog (13, 17, 18, 20, 21, 28, 42, 48)

bone (42)

doghouse (17, 28)

candlestick (13)

Teacher: Enlarge or reduce copies of the patterns to vary the sizes of the cutouts. Laminate or cover them with clear self-sticking paper for sturdiness. Use them as cutouts or as templates for tracing on felt or other fabrics.

airplane (19, 21)

fish (15, 18, 20, 21)

lizard (19, 21, 30)

tooth (19)

Teacher: Enlarge or reduce copies of the patterns to vary the sizes of the cutouts. Laminate or cover them with clear self-sticking paper for sturdiness. Use them as cutouts or as templates for tracing on felt or other fabrics.

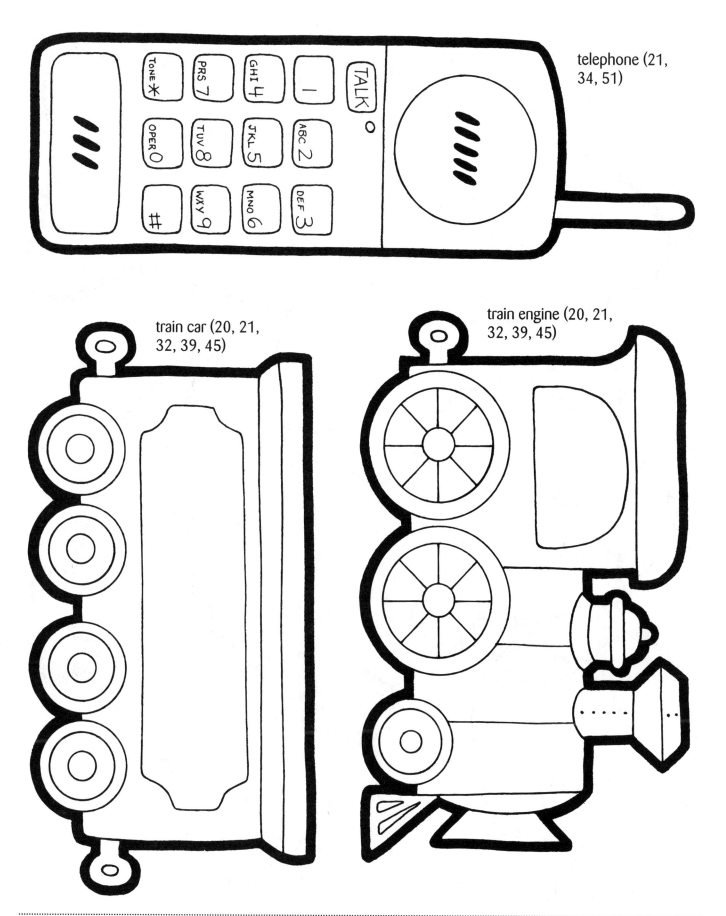

telephone (21, 34, 51)

train car (20, 21, 32, 39, 45)

train engine (20, 21, 32, 39, 45)

TONE ✳ PRS 7 GHI 4 1 TALK
OPER 0 TUV 8 JKL 5 ABC 2
WXY 9 MNO 6 DEF 3

Teacher: Enlarge or reduce copies of the patterns to vary the sizes of the cutouts. Laminate or cover them with clear self-sticking paper for sturdiness. Use them as cutouts or as templates for tracing on felt or other fabrics.

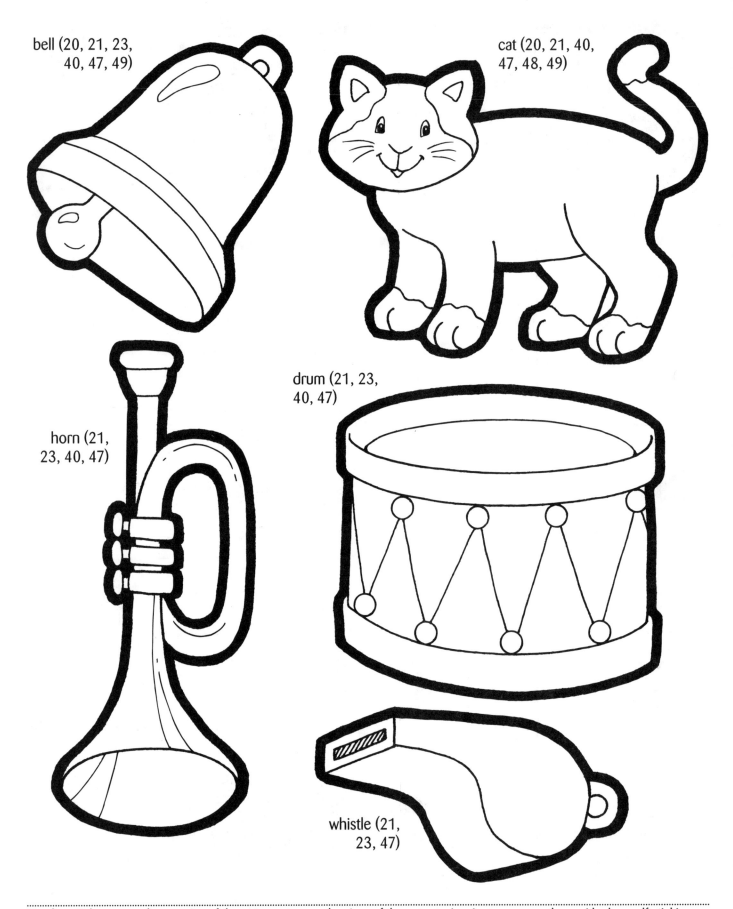

bell (20, 21, 23, 40, 47, 49)

cat (20, 21, 40, 47, 48, 49)

horn (21, 23, 40, 47)

drum (21, 23, 40, 47)

whistle (21, 23, 47)

Teacher: Enlarge or reduce copies of the patterns to vary the sizes of the cutouts. Laminate or cover them with clear self-sticking paper for sturdiness. Use them as cutouts or as templates for tracing on felt or other fabrics.

56

star (26)

circus
stand (25)

rooster (27, 48)

hen (46)

Teacher: Enlarge or reduce copies of the patterns to vary the sizes of the cutouts. Laminate or cover them with clear self-sticking paper for sturdiness. Use them as cutouts or as templates for tracing on felt or other fabrics.

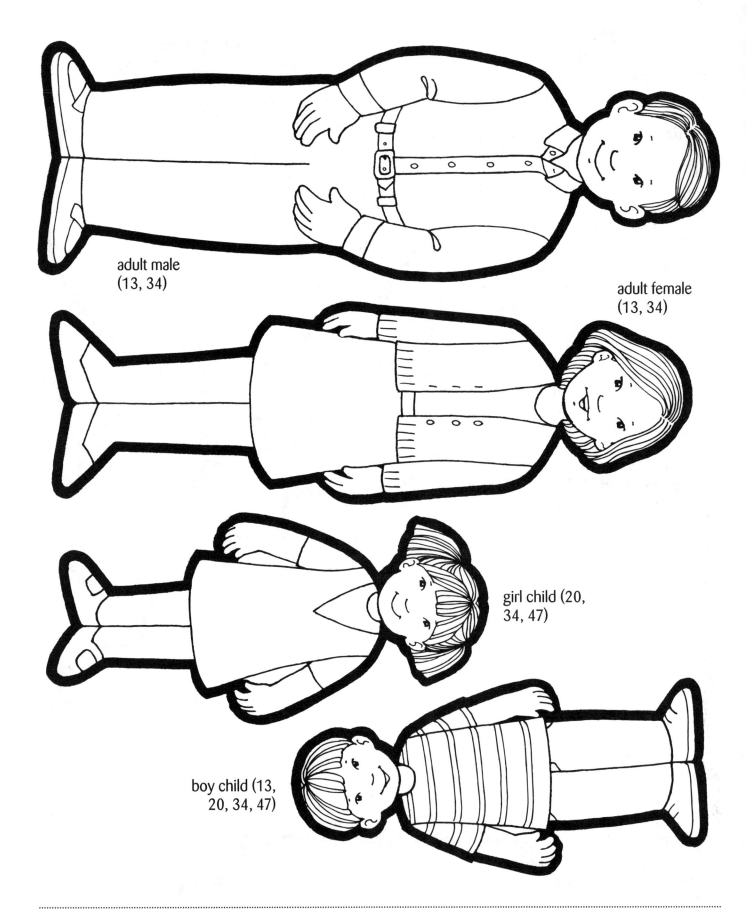

adult male
(13, 34)

adult female
(13, 34)

girl child (20, 34, 47)

boy child (13, 20, 34, 47)

Teacher: Enlarge or reduce copies of the patterns to vary the sizes of the cutouts. Laminate or cover them with clear self-sticking paper for sturdiness. Use them as cutouts or as templates for tracing on felt or other fabrics.

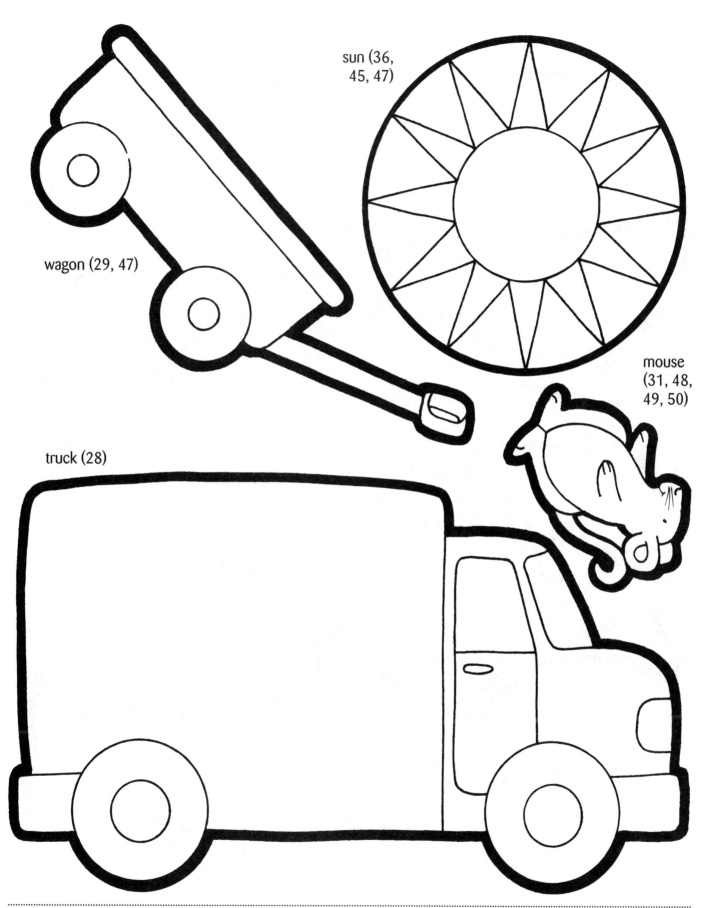

sun (36, 45, 47)

wagon (29, 47)

mouse (31, 48, 49, 50)

truck (28)

Teacher: Enlarge or reduce copies of the patterns to vary the sizes of the cutouts. Laminate or cover them with clear self-sticking paper for sturdiness. Use them as cutouts or as templates for tracing on felt or other fabrics.

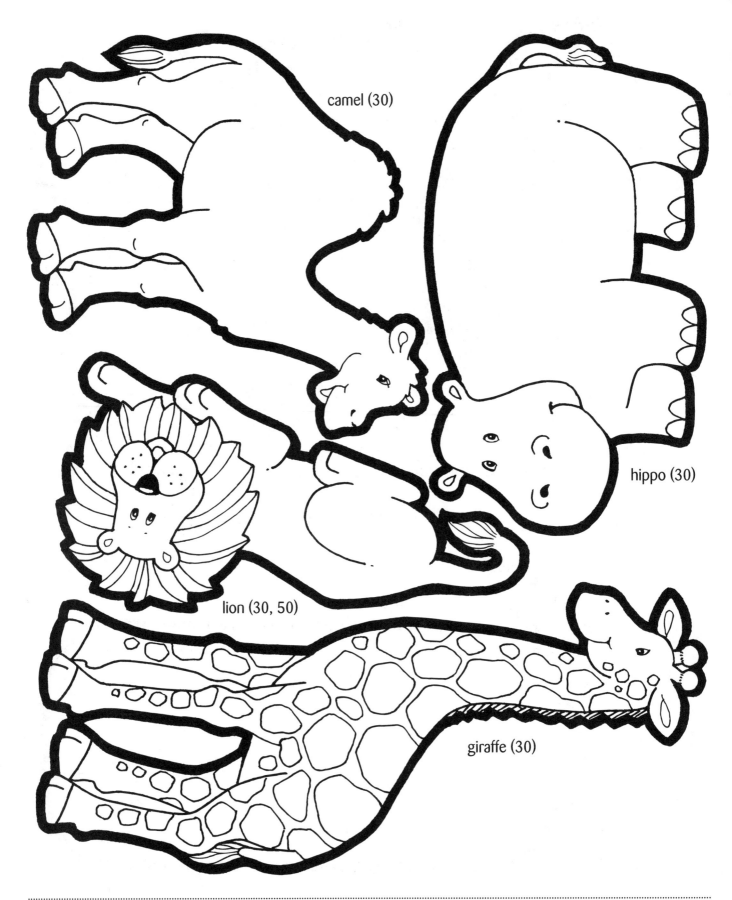

camel (30)

hippo (30)

lion (30, 50)

giraffe (30)

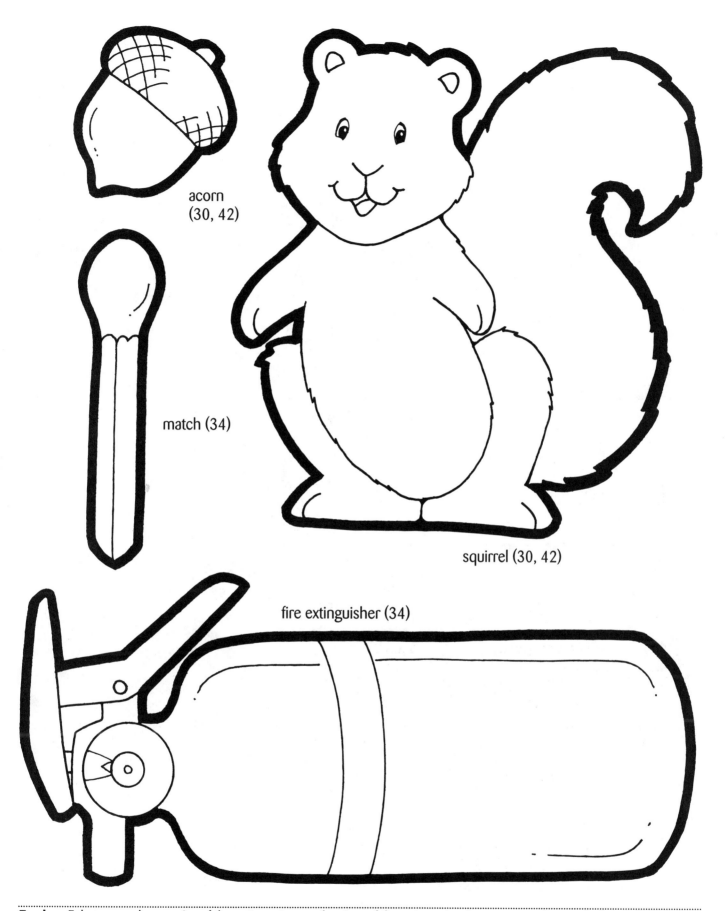

acorn
(30, 42)

match (34)

squirrel (30, 42)

fire extinguisher (34)

Teacher: Enlarge or reduce copies of the patterns to vary the sizes of the cutouts. Laminate or cover them with clear self-sticking paper for sturdiness. Use them as cutouts or as templates for tracing on felt or other fabrics.

traffic signs (35)

Teacher: Enlarge or reduce copies of the patterns to vary the sizes of the cutouts. Laminate or cover them with clear self-sticking paper for sturdiness. Use them as cutouts or as templates for tracing on felt or other fabrics.

J330001 Using Flannelboards to Teach Readiness Skills

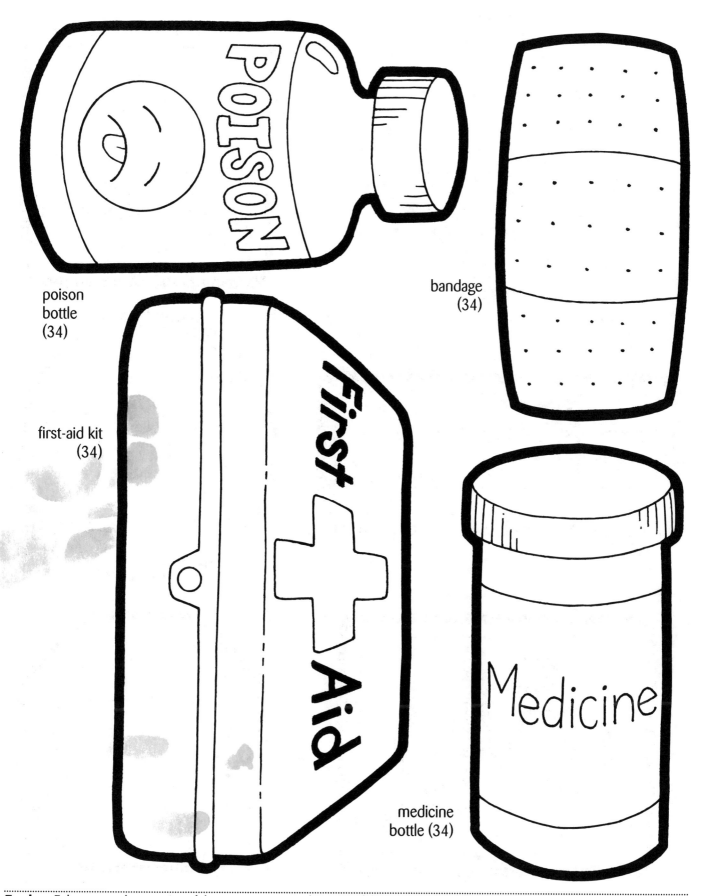

poison
bottle
(34)

bandage
(34)

first-aid kit
(34)

medicine
bottle (34)

Teacher: Enlarge or reduce copies of the patterns to vary the sizes of the cutouts. Laminate or cover them with clear self-sticking paper for sturdiness. Use them as cutouts or as templates for tracing on felt or other fabrics.

flower (45)

scissors (44)

pencil (44)

glue (44)

GLUE

clay pot (45)

Teacher: Enlarge or reduce copies of the patterns to vary the sizes of the cutouts. Laminate or cover them with clear self-sticking paper for sturdiness. Use them as cutouts or as templates for tracing on felt or other fabrics.